Annie's Pictures

by Jane Manners
illustrated by Diane Greenseid

Harcourt

Orlando Boston Dallas Chicago San Diego

Visit *The Learning Site!*

www.harcourtschool.com

Annie had been waiting all morning for her grandmother to arrive. Grandma's visits were always special.

"Hi, Grandma!" Annie called out.

DRAKE

Her grandmother smiled and gave her
a big hug. Then she handed Annie a box.

"This is for you," she said.

Annie was so excited. "What is it?"
she asked, studying the box.

"Open it and find out," her
grandmother said.

Annie ripped off the wrapping paper.
Inside the box was a camera! "I picked it
out just for you," said Annie's grandmother.
"I thought you might like to take some
pictures of your farm."

Annie's grandmother showed her how
to load the film. "Now you're ready to go."
"Thank you, Grandma!" said Annie. Then
she looked through the camera at her
grandmother. "Smile," she said.

Annie and her grandmother walked around the farm. Annie saw an orange and yellow leaf fall from a tree. Annie took a picture before the leaf hit the ground.

A cool breeze sent all the leaves on the ground swirling through the air. Pixie, Annie's old cat, sat watching the leaves fly around her. *What a great picture,* thought Annie.

"Look at the sky," said her grandmother.
"Those birds are headed south for the
winter."

Annie took a picture quickly before
the birds flew out of sight.

Annie's mother came out of the house.

"Mom, what are you making?" Annie asked, sniffing the air.

"I made a special pie for your grandma," she said.

"Smile, Mom!" Annie said as she snapped a picture.

Then they rode up the winding path to see what Annie's father was doing. Annie wanted to take more pictures, but the ride was too bumpy.

At the top of the hill, Annie's father was busy putting apples into baskets and boxes. "Look at all the apples you picked, Dad," Annie said, counting the bushels near the road.

Annie was about to take another picture when something caught her eye.

It was two chipmunks. They raced away. Annie followed them down the path, but they darted through the grass toward the woods.

Those little chipmunks are too fast for me, Annie thought, as she stepped over a pumpkin.

Annie decided to take a picture of the pumpkins instead.

It was easy to take pictures of the pumpkins. The pumpkins didn't run like those chipmunks did. They didn't fly away like the birds or swirl through the air like the leaves.

Annie took pictures of every single pumpkin in the patch until the camera made a funny noise. Then she heard the sound of the film rewinding. She had finished the whole roll of film.

The next morning, Annie put in new film. She was taking Grandma to visit her second-grade class. Now she could take pictures of this special day!